Wilton CELEBRATE!®

A Christmas Collection of Festive Foods & Desserts

Entertaining is an integral part of the holiday season. From children's parties, office gatherings, open houses to family festivities—they all have one thing in common—food! But, the age-old question is—what to serve? You want to create that eye-appealing, appetite-teasing dish; that beautifully decorated, delightfully-delicious dessert. Sound overwhelming? Not so. Just leave it to us . . .

Celebrate! is all about creating fabulous food that you will enjoy preparing, just as much as sharing. Our "Festive Foods" section covers everything from breakfast through dinner, with snacks in-between! "Delectable Desserts" offers a sweet ending to the perfect meal. The "Delightful Decorating" section is filled with spectacular projects that let you get creative. The collection of taste-tempters in "Colorful Candy & Cookies" includes projects suitable for the whole family. "Jolly Gingerbread" helps you express this festive season with fabulous table-toppers. Think you couldn't possibly have enough time? Well, think again . . .

Our special gift to you this season is the gift of extra time. Look for our Time-Saver Tip and Time-Saver Project symbols throughout this book. They designate recipes and projects that can be made with some welcome short-cuts that will have you in and out of the kitchen quickly. So come on, take off your apron, join the party and CELEBRATE!

Learn cake decorating the Wilton way!
Sign up for a Wilton class near you.

800-942-8881

CONTENTS

For casual table decorations, place a votive candle in the center of a Singles!™ Star Pan. Fill around candle with miniature pinecones, nuts in shell or holiday candies. Bright idea!

Spread a little holiday cheer
with these awesome appetizers!

Chicken or Liver Paté

2 Packets Unflavored Gelatin
(4 Teaspoons)

¼ Cup Cool Broth (Beef for Liver,
Chicken for chicken)

1 lb. Liverwurst or 2 Whole
Chicken Breasts (1½ - 2 lbs.)

¼ Medium Onion,
Coarsely Chopped

1 Clove Garlic, Coarsely Chopped

1 Tablespoon
Dijon Mustard

½ Teaspoon Nutmeg

2 Tablespoons Brandy

½ Cup (4 oz., 1 Stick) Butter
Slightly Softened

4 oz. Cream Cheese

Salt and Pepper to Taste

Festive Foods

To prepare chicken; place chicken breasts in a small amount of water and simmer or microwave until just done; do not overcook. Cool; skin and debone. Reserve broth.

Soften gelatin in broth; heat until dissolved. Set aside. Lightly oil mold.

Place liverwurst or cooked coarsely chopped chicken in food processor fitted with metal blade. Process until chopped. Add onion, garlic, remaining seasonings and brandy. Process until smooth. Add cream cheese and butter, process; add gelatin mixture and process until smooth. Taste for seasonings; add salt and pepper to taste. Some brands of liverwurst will be very salty, you may not need additional salt.

Place in prepared mold; tap down and smooth tops. Chill overnight until firm. To unmold, carefully run small knife around edges of molds and release.

Makes 3-4 molds

Purchase cheese balls or spreads at the supermarket. Line Singles!™ molds with plastic wrap, press cheese mix firmly into mold. Unmold and garnish. Perfect for serving or hostess gift.

Festive Foods

CHRISTMAS
CAVIAR
CANES

Cheerful appetizers add color and whimsy to any holiday buffet!

Caviar Canes

5 Large Eggs, Hard-Boiled   ½ Cup Sour Cream
6 Tablespoons Butter, Melted   1 (2 oz.) Jar Red Caviar
Salt and Pepper, to Taste

Line molds with plastic wrap. In food processor fitted with steel blade (or by hand) finely chop eggs. With processor running, pour butter through feed tube. Process just until mixed. Season with salt and pepper to taste.

Fill molds with egg mixture; refrigerate 2 hours or until firm. Unmold; spread with sour cream. Chill 1 hour. Stripe with caviar. Serve with crackers.

Makes 2 canes.

CHECKLIST

Wilton Products
Singles!™ Candy Cane Molds

Ingredients
Hard-Boiled Eggs
Butter
Salt and Pepper
Sour Cream
Red Caviar

Use your Wilton Nesting Star Cookie Cutters and refrigerated cookie dough to create an easy, edible tree centerpiece. Cut out cookies and bake, as directed. Stack stars with largest at bottom and smallest at top. Decorate with Wilton Decorating Gels. Perfect family activity!

Make these star toasts in a twinkling! Simply flatten bread with a rolling pin, cut with Wilton Nesting Star Cookie Cutters and toast for 7-8 minutes in a 400° oven.

TIME SAVER TIP

COFFEE CAKES

Take a break from shopping with fragrant, fresh-from-the-oven treats!

Coffee Cake

2 (1 lb.) Loaves of Frozen Sweet Bread Dough, Thawed

$^1/_4$ Cup ($^1/_2$ Stick) Butter or Margarine

$^1/_4$ Cup Sugar

1 Tablespoon Cinnamon

Thaw bread. On floured surface, roll each loaf into a 5 x 12 in. oblong shape. Cover with plastic wrap; let rest 15 minutes. Roll each piece into approximately a 16 x 9 in. rectangle. Melt butter, brush on top of dough. Combine sugar and cinnamon, sprinkle evenly over butter. Starting on long side, roll each piece into a cylinder, pinch seams. Cut into $^3/_4$ in. cinnamon rolls. Spray pan with vegetable pan spray. Arrange rolls, cut side down in pan. Let raise about 45 minutes. Preheat oven to 350°. Bake 35-40 minutes. Cool 20 minutes. Remove from pan; drizzle with glaze. For glaze: Mix $^1/_2$ cup confectioners' sugar, 2 teaspoons water in small bowl.

Makes 10 servings.

Petite Cinnamon Loaves

1 Package (1 lb. 14 oz.) Cinnamon Swirl Bread Mix

1 Teaspoon Vanilla Extract

$^1/_4$ Cup Chopped Pecans or Walnuts

$^1/_4$ Cup Raisins

Preheat oven to 350°. Line pan with baking cups. Follow package mixing instructions, adding vanilla. Stir in nuts and raisins. Bake 20-25 minutes or until toothpick inserted in center comes out clean.

Makes 9 loaves.

CHECKLIST

CINNAMON TREE
Wilton Products
Treeliteful Pan
Ingredients
Sweet Bread Dough
Butter or Margarine
Sugar
Cinnamon

PETITE LOAVES
Wilton Products
Petite Loaf Pan
Petite Loaf Baking Cups
Ingredients
Cinnamon Swirl Bread Mix
Vanilla Extract
Chopped Pecans or Walnuts
Raisins

Use our Petite Loaf Pan to create individual breads for your guests. It's ideal for gift giving, too!

Take it easy! Substitute two packages of refrigerated cinnamon rolls for the Cinnamon Tree recipe.

TIME SAVER · TIP

9

MORNING
MAGIC

Wake up to a merry morning with Santa's favorite breakfast!

CHECKLIST

Wilton Products

Smiling Santa Pan

Ingredients

Biscuit Mix

Light Brown Sugar

Ground Cinnamon

Undiluted Evaporated Milk or Evaporated Skim Milk

Bananas

Vegetable Oil

Eggs

Treats made with Wilton's Smiling Santa Pan appeal to kids of all ages. Create a quick decorated cake using your favorite mix, candy features and a whipped cream beard. Yummy!

Santa Pancake

2 Cups Biscuit Mix	2 Teaspoons Ground Cinnamon
2 Tablespoons Packed Light Brown Sugar	1½ Bananas, Mashed
1½ Cups (12 oz. can) Undiluted Evaporated Milk or Evaporated Skim Milk	2 Tablespoons Vegetable Oil
	2 Eggs

Place Santa Pan in oven; heat pan and oven to 450°. In large bowl, combine biscuit mix, sugar, cinnamon, evaporated milk, bananas, oil and eggs. Beat or whisk until smooth. When oven is heated, remove pan. CAUTION: pan will be very hot. Spray pan with vegetable pan spray. Pour 2 cups of batter in pan. Pour in circle to cover pan evenly. Push to edges if necessary. Return to oven and bake 6-8 minutes or until top is dry and edges are brown. Top will not be brown. Invert on serving dish. Repeat for next pancake. Batter may be stored overnight in refrigerator. Stir before using. Garnish with raisin eyes, cherry nose, jelly hat and confectioners' sugar. If star fruit is available in your area, use as garnish. Cut pieces of waxed paper to cover face when dusting with sugar.

Makes 2 large pancakes, 2-4 servings.

Make all your batter a day or two ahead of time. Make pancakes up to an hour before serving. To keep warm: put on cookie sheet, cover loosely with foil, place in 250° oven. Garnish just before serving.

TIME SAVER · TIP

STRATA
STAR

This savory, make-ahead dish is a "stellar performer" at Christmas brunch!

CHECKLIST

Wilton Products

Star Pan

Ingredients

White Bread

Shredded Colby and Monterey Jack Cheeses

Italian Sausage

Sweet Red Peppers

Broccoli Florets

Eggs

Milk

Dijon Mustard

Salt

Crushed Red Pepper Flakes

Onion and Garlic Powder

Pepper

The Wilton Star Pan adds sparkle to holiday parties. Use to create an ice mold for your punch bowl. Partially fill pan with water or punch ingredients; add fruits, such as cherries, orange, lemon, or lime slices and freeze. Heavenly!

Star Strata

13 Slices White Bread

³/₄ Cup Each Shredded Colby and Monterey Jack Cheeses

12 Eggs, Lightly Beaten

³/₄ Cup Milk

1 Teaspoon Dijon Mustard

¹/₂ Teaspoon Salt

¹/₄ Teaspoon Crushed Red Pepper Flakes

¹/₄ Teaspoon Each Onion and Garlic Powder

Pepper to Taste

¹/₂ Cup Sliced Cooked Italian Sausage

¹/₄ Cup Sweet Red Peppers, Roasted and Drained or Fresh and Diced

¹/₂ Cup Broccoli Florets

Preheat oven to 350°F. Mold foil over back of star pan, line star pan with molded foil and spray lightly with pan spray. Remove crusts from 5 slices of bread, cut into triangles and stand up along star points. Cube remaining bread in ¹/₂ in. pieces. Combine eggs, milk, mustard, salt, crushed red pepper, garlic and onion powders and pepper. Sprinkle half the bread and cheese in prepared pan; repeat layers. Top with sausage, red pepper and broccoli. Pour egg mixture over bread. Bake 30-35 minutes or until puffy and golden brown. Let set 10 minutes. Remove from pan.

Serves 8-10.

Strata may be prepared one day ahead and baked the day of serving or bake in advance and refrigerate or freeze and reheat on serving day. To reheat, bake at 350°F for 20-25 minutes.

TASTY
TREE
TRIMMINGS

Two heart-warming "tree-ts" guaranteed to satisfy picky palates!

CHECKLIST

SPRUCED UP PIZZA

Wilton Products

12 in. Non-Stick Tree
Tart/Quiche Pan

Ingredients

Refrigerator Pizza Crust

Frozen Kale or Other Greens

Italian Sausage

Mozzarella Cheese

CHEESE POTATO TREES

Wilton Products

12 in. Non-Stick Tree
Tart/Quiche Pan

Ingredients

Mashed Potatoes

Sour Cream

Grated Cheddar Cheese

Salt and Pepper

Paprika

Bacon

The Wilton Non-Stick Tree
Tart/Quiche Pan makes holiday
brunch time festive.
Fruit tarts, quiches
and entrées are
ready-to-serve
on the remove-
able pan bottom.

Spruced Up Pizza

1 (10 oz.) Refrigerator
Pizza Crust

1 (10 oz.) Frozen Kale
or Other Greens, Thawed
and Well Drained

3-4 oz. Italian Sausage,
Sliced and Sautéed

6 oz. Mozzarella
Cheese, Sliced Thin

Preheat oven to 400°F. Press pizza
crust into pan. Bake for 10 minutes,
remove. Arrange cheese slices
over crust. Place greens and
sausage over cheese.
Return to oven and bake
an additional 20 minutes,
or until pizza is browned
and cheese melted.

**Makes 12 appetizer
or 3 main
dish servings.**

14

Easy Cheese Potato Trees

5 Cups Prepared Mashed
Potatoes: 2 (1 lb. 4 oz.)
Packages Fresh Mashed
Potatoes or Your Favorite
Recipe Made with 2 lbs.
Potatoes

1 Cup Sour Cream

1½ Cups Grated
Cheddar Cheese

4 Green Onions
Salt and Pepper to Taste
1 Teaspoon Paprika
Bacon Curls for Garnish

Preheat oven to 400°F. Chop white part of green onion, reserve tops for garnish. Combine all ingredients except paprika and bacon curls. Lightly spray Tree Tart Pan with vegetable pan spray. Spread potato mixture in prepared pan. Sprinkle with paprika. Bake 20-25 minutes or until brown. To remove rim, place tart pan on large can and press down on rim. Transfer potatoes, on tart pan bottom to serving plate. Garnish.

Makes 6-8 servings.

For more smashing mashed potatoes, leave on the peelings (they're easier to make and more nutritious too!). Or, cook with garlic cloves for a wonderful flavor treat.

TIME SAVER TIP

HOLIDAY
CHICKEN
SALAD

Decorate your party table with this tastefully trimmed tree!

CHECKLIST

Wilton Products
Treeliteful Pan

Ingredients
Roasted Chicken
Celery
Red Seedless Grapes
Walnuts
Sour Cream
Light Mayonnaise
Lemon
Fresh Rosemary
Salt and Pepper

Use "Treeliteful" to turn any pasta salad, rice or couscous recipe into holiday fare. Pack recipe firmly into plastic wrap-lined pan. Invert onto serving platter and garnish. Festive!

Chicken Salad

2 Chickens (Approximately 2-2$\frac{1}{2}$ lbs. Each)

5 Ribs Celery, Chopped

1$\frac{1}{2}$ lbs. (3 Cups) Red Seedless Grapes, Halved

1 (10 oz.) Package Walnuts, 1$\frac{1}{2}$ Cups, Chopped

1$\frac{1}{2}$ Cups Sour Cream

1$\frac{1}{2}$ Cups Light Mayonnaise

Juice From $\frac{1}{2}$ Lemon

$\frac{1}{2}$ Teaspoon Chopped Fresh Rosemary

Salt and Pepper to Taste

Skin, bone and coarsely chop chicken. In a large bowl, combine chicken, celery, grapes and walnuts. In a separate bowl combine sour cream, mayonnaise, lemon juice and seasonings, taste and adjust salt and pepper. Combine with chicken mixture. Line Treeliteful Pan with plastic wrap. Spoon salad into pan. Pack down firmly with back of spoon and cover with plastic wrap. Place cookie sheet over salad and press. Refrigerate one hour or overnight. Remove top plastic wrap and place platter on top of mold and invert.

Makes 12 main dish servings.

No need to fuss with cooking the chicken yourself—use "supermarket" rotisserie chickens instead. Perfect for entertaining on short notice. Hint: Fresh rosemary makes the ideal holiday garnish.

TIME SAVER TIP

SHIMMERING SALAD STARS

Tangy, tasty salads designed to make your holidays sparkle!

CHECKLIST

Wilton Products
Singles!™ Star Mold

Ingredients
Cranberries
Oranges
Crushed Pineapple
Sugar
Unflavored Gelatin

Cranberry Salad Stars

½ lb. Fresh Cranberries   2¼ Cups Sugar
2 Oranges   1 Envelope Unflavored Gelatin
8 oz. Crushed Pineapple

Peel oranges, reserve peel from one half of orange. Grind or process with metal blade in food processor cranberries, oranges and reserved peel; add crushed pineapple. Strain and press juice out of fruit. Add sugar to fruit. Dissolve gelatin in one cup of cold juice. Heat the remaining juice; add gelatin mixture, stir until dissolved. When cool, add to fruit mixture. Rinse star pans with cold water and pour mixture into molds. Refrigerate overnight. Unmold by dipping to rim in warm water for 5-10 seconds. Unmold on serving dish. Garnish with fresh cranberries, mint sprigs and orange zest. To make orange curls, wind zest around a drinking straw and refrigerate 1-2 hours.

Makes 6 stars.

Create "Celestial Corn Cakes" by adding 1 can well-drained corn; garlic, cumin or chili powder to taste to your favorite corn bread recipe. Bake in well-greased Singles!™ Star Molds—guaranteed to be a year-round favorite!

It's quick and easy to substitute the following for fresh cranberries: dissolve one 3 oz. package cranberry gelatin according to package directions. Add one 12 oz. package ready-to-use "CranFruit for Chicken" relish. Follow remaining steps in directions for swift success!

TIME SAVER • TIP

19

Hearty Bean Soup

1 Large Onion, Chopped

1 (8 oz.) Can Sauerkraut, Drained

2 Tablespoons Olive Oil

1 (14 oz.) Can Chicken Broth

1 (8 oz.) Can Whole Tomatoes

1 (15 oz.) Can Navy or Great Northern Beans

8 oz. Kielbasa Sausage, Sliced and Sautéed

In a 2-quart saucepan, sauté onion and sauerkraut in oil until soft, but not browned. Add remaining ingredients except sausage. Simmer 30 minutes. Add sautéed sausage and serve. The soup tastes even better when made and stored in refrigerator overnight.

Makes 4 servings.

LITTLE
LOVES

Raise a toast
to these "Souper-Stars"—
Beer is their secret ingredient.

Beer Batter Bread

3 Cups Flour	1½ Teaspoon Salt
1 Tablespoons, Plus 1½ Teaspoons Baking Powder	12 oz. Beer

Preheat oven to 350°F. Spray Mini Star Pan
with vegetable pan spray. Combine flour,
baking powder, and salt in large bowl. Add
beer and stir until all flour is mixed in.
Spoon into prepared pan. Fill each cavity
½ inch from top. Bake for 20 to 25 minutes
or until brown. Remove from pan and serve
warm. May be reheated in microwave.

Makes 10-12 Stars

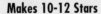

CHECKLIST

BEER BREAD
Wilton Products
Mini Star Pan
Ingredients
Flour
Baking Powder
Salt
Beer

BEAN SOUP
Ingredients
Onion
Sauerkraut
Olive Oil
Chicken Broth
Tomatoes
Navy or Great Northern Beans
Kielbasa Sausage

The Wilton Mini Star Pan makes it
easy to make individual gelatin
desserts. Add prepared whipped
topping, diced fruit and nuts to
partially set gelatin.
Pour into pan and
refrigerate until
firm. Unmold
onto dessert plates
and garnish. Starry, starry night!

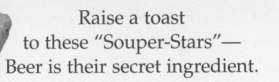

CHRISTMAS
CRIMSON
SALAD

Put this pretty poinsettia on your table
and the compliments will fly!

CHECKLIST

Wilton Products
Poinsettia Pan

Ingredients
Cranberry Gelatin
Jellied Cranberry Sauce
Frozen Whipped Topping
Cream Cheese
Nuts

Our new Poinsettia Pan is
perfect for holiday cakes,
molded candy,
gelatin salads,
ice molds...
You'll be
suprised at how
many uses you'll find!

Cranberry Salad

1 Package (6 oz.) Cranberry
Gelatin Dessert Mix

1 (16 oz.) Can Jellied
Cranberry Sauce

1 (12 oz.) Package Frozen Whipped
Topping, Thawed

For Garnish:
1 (3 oz.) Package Cream Cheese
1/4 Cup Finely Chopped Nuts

Dissolve gelatin in 2 cups boiling water, add cranberry sauce.
Break sauce up with a whisk. Rinse Poinsettia Pan with cold water,
pour half gelatin mixture into pan, refrigerate until set. Refrigerate
remaining gelatin until the thickness of egg whites. With a whisk
mix gelatin and thawed topping until smooth. Pour on top of
gelatin in pan. Gelatin should be set in pan before top layer is
added. Refrigerate until set, 6 hours or overnight. Unmold by
carefully running a small spatula or knife around edge of mold,
then dipping pan up to rim in warm water for 10 seconds.

For garnish: roll cream cheese into balls, then roll in chopped
nuts. Refrigerate until ready to serve. Garnish with lemon leaves
if desired.

Makes 12 servings.

Delectable Desserts

FRESH
FRUIT
TARTS

A delicious dessert duo that adds a flair to holiday happenings!

CHECKLIST

Wilton Products
Mini Tree Non-Stick Tart/
Quiche Pan

Ingredients
Prepared Pie Crusts

PEAR TART
Pears
Sugar
Apple Jelly

CRANBERRY TART
Fresh Cranberries
Dried Cranberries
Cranberry Gelatin Dessert
Sugar
Oranges
Triple Sec

Bake your favorite sugar
cookie dough recipe and
pat into Mini Tree Non-Stick
Tart/Quiche Pan. Bake until
golden. Unmold and cool.
Fill wih your favorite ice
cream, yogurt or
sherbet.

Tart Crust

2 Pkgs. (16 oz.) Prepared Pie Crusts, or Two Recipes of Double Pie Crust

Preheat oven to 375°F. Cut each crust into four triangles. Press into tart pans. Trim top by pressing with fingers or roll rolling pin across top. Prick crust with fork. Bake for 10-12 minutes or until browned. Remove and cool.

Pear Filling

3 Fresh Pears (1½ lbs.)   ½ Cup Water
¾ Cup Sugar   ¼ Cup Apple Jelly, Melted

Halve and core pears (a melon baller works great for this). Slice crosswise, starting at stem end, into thin slices. Combine pears, sugar and water; cook in a shallow pan or dish on stovetop or in microwave for 6-10 minutes or just until tender. Pears should be slightly firm and not lose their shape. Set aside until cool, or prepare a day ahead, cover and refrigerate overnight. Arrange in baked shell. Brush with melted jelly. Garnish with whole cooked or dried cranberries. Tarts are best assembled the day they are to be served.

Cranberry Filling

12 Oz. Package Fresh Cranberries   1 Teaspoon Orange Zest
⅓ Cup Dried Cranberries   1 Tablespoon Triple Sec or Other
¼ Cup (approx. ½ pkg.) Cranberry   Orange Flavored Liqueur (Optional)
Gelatin Dessert   Orange Curls for Garnish
¾ Cup Sugar

Place all ingredients except liqueur and garnish into 2 quart pan or bowl. Cook over medium heat or microwave for 10-15 minutes, until cranberries are tender but do not lose their shape. Add liqueur. Let cool to room temperature. Fill tart shells, garnish with orange curls.

Makes 8 tarts.

Shells may be baked ahead and kept in an air-tight container for 2-3 days or frozen for up to a week.

FESTIVE
FROZEN
DELIGHTS

Turn ice cream and tempting toppings into a delightfully delicious dessert!

Ice Cream Molds

1 Quart Ice Cream or Frozen Yogurt

1 (12 oz.) Jar Fudge Sauce

Whipped Cream or Frozen Whipped Topping

Cherry Sauce

Wilton Red Cake Sparkles™

Soften ice cream at room temperature for 15 minutes; stir until smooth, but not melted. Line pan cavities with plastic wrap; allow enough to completely wrap molds. Press ice cream into mold, do not overfill. Fold excess plastic over to wrap. Freeze overnight. If you need to make extras, ice cream can be removed from mold as soon as filled and wrapped. Place on chilled cookie sheet and freeze.

When ready to serve: Place sauce onto serving plate, add molded ice cream or yogurt, top with more sauce. For Stocking, sprinkle with cake sparkles; and add tip 21 whipped cream cuff. Garnish with Holly Sprinkle Decorations.

Makes 4 molds.

CHECKLIST

Wilton Products

Singles!™ Tree, Stocking and Star Molds

Red Cake Sparkles™

Holly Sprinkle Decorations

Tip 21

Ingredients

Ice Cream or Frozen Yogurt

Fudge Sauce

Whipped Cream or Frozen Whipped Topping

Cherry Sauce

Add a new dimension to your next sheet cake! Bake 3-4 cakes in Singles!™ Pans (Stars or Hearts are a great choice!) Add Singles!™ cakes to sheet cake. For easy icing of small cakes, place on cookie sheet, ice, refrigerate 30-45 minutes, then lift with spatula to sheet cake or serving plate.

MERRY
MERINGUE
TARTS!

Tempt your guests with these melt-in-your-mouth meringue marvels!

Cookie Crust

$^1/_2$ Cup Butter	1 Tablespoon Milk
1 Cup Sugar	1 Teaspoon Vanilla Extract
1 Egg	$^1/_4$ Teaspoon Salt
$1^3/_4$ Cups Flour	

Cream butter and sugar, add egg and mix. Add remaining ingredients and mix until smooth. Refrigerate dough for 2 hours.

Preheat oven to 350°F. Press about 3 tablespoons dough into each tree tart. Prick bottom with a fork. Bake 8-10 minutes or until very light brown. Remove; reduce oven temperature to 275°F; fill with Meringue Mixture. Return to oven and bake 45-50 minutes or until lightly browned and dry.

Makes 12 tarts.

Meringue Filling

4 Teaspoons Wilton Meringue Powder	$^1/_2$ Teaspoon Orange Flavor
4 Tablespoons Water	$^3/_4$ Cup Coarsely Chopped Fresh Cranberries
$^1/_2$ Cup Sugar	$^1/_2$ Cup Chopped Pecans

Beat meringue powder with water, sugar and orange flavor on high speed 4-5 minutes or until stiff peaks form. Stir in cranberries and nuts. VARIATION: Replace cranberries with chocolate chips.

TO MAKE CHOCOLATE CHIP MERINGUE COOKIES (shown on page 31): Follow above recipe for Meringue filling and use following baking directions:
Preheat oven to 275°F. Line cookie sheet with parchment paper. Drop by tablespoons onto prepared pan. Bake 55-60 minutes or until lightly browned and dry.

Makes approximately 2 dozen.

MARZIPAN
MERINGUES

These winter-white wonders are amazingly easy to make!

CHECKLIST

Wilton Products

Cookie Sheet

Meringue Powder

White Cake Sparkles™

Ingredients

Almond Paste

Grated Orange Peel

Water

Sugar

Orange Flavor

Wilton's Meringue Powder is perfect for making Royal and boiled icing.

Meringue Cookies

1 Can (8 oz.) Almond Paste

4 Teaspoons Grated Orange Peel, Chopped Fine

4 Teaspoons Meringue Powder

4 Tablespoons Water

$1/2$ Cup Sugar

$1/2$ Teaspoon Orange Flavor

Preheat oven to 250°. Line baking sheet with parchment paper. Knead almond paste and orange peel until well blended. Divide in half; roll each half with fingertips into 15 in. long roll. Cut into $3/4$ in. pieces; roll each into a ball. Beat meringue, water, sugar and orange flavor at high speed 4-5 minutes or until stiff peaks form. Coat marzipan balls with meringue, covering completely. Place on prepared baking sheets. Check to be sure marzipan balls are completely covered with meringue. Bake 55-60 minutes or until crisp. Cool completely on rack. Sprinkle with white Cake Sparkles.

Makes 2-3 dozen cookies.

Note: See page 29 for Chocolate Chip Meringues Recipe.

TIME SAVER · RECIPE ·

Delectable Desserts

TEMPTING
TART
TRIO

Elegant, yet easy, guest-pleasing festive desserts!

Wilton Products

Non-Stick Tart/Quiche Pans: Tree, 4x14 in. Rectangle, 9" Round

Ingredients

Pie Crust Recipe

Cream Cheese

Sugar

Vanilla Extract

Egg

Flour

Cherry Pie Filling

Peaches

Apricot Jam

Pears

Caramel Sauce

Nuts

Tarts

BASIC TART (makes 1)

1 Single Pie Crust Recipe

1 (8 oz.) Package Cream Cheese, Softened

$1/2$ Cup Sugar

1 Teaspoon Vanilla

1 Egg, Lightly Beaten

1 Tablespoon Flour

FILLINGS

1 (16 oz.) Can Cherry Pie Filling

3 Fresh Peaches, Sliced

$1/4$ Cup Apricot Jam, Melted and Strained

2 Fresh Pears, Peeled, Cored and Sliced

Caramel Sauce, Nuts

Preheat oven to 375°. Roll out dough to $1/8$ in. thick and 2 in. larger than pan. Press pie crust into bottom and sides of pan and prick bottom with fork. Bake 10-12 minutes or until light golden brown and crisp. Remove from oven. Reduce oven temperature to 350°. In mixer bowl beat cream cheese, sugar, vanilla and egg until smooth. Add flour and blend well. Pour filling into warm crust and bake 20 minutes or until filling is set. Cool tart in pan on rack. Top Tree with cherries, Rectangle with pears and caramel sauce, Round with peaches glazed with jam. Use any fresh or canned fruit on this cheese base.

Refrigerate if not serving within one hour.

Each serves 8-10.

With fluted edges and a convenient removable bottom, Wilton Non-Stick Tart/Quiche Pans help you serve beautifully and clean up easily this party season.

TREE-MENDOUS
BROWNIE
TREAT

Trim this "cool" tree with your favorite sundae toppings!

CHECKLIST

Wilton Products

Treeliteful Pan

Cake Board

Fanci-Foil Wrap

Rainbow Nonpareils Sprinkle Decorations

Ingredients

Eggs

Sugar

Butter or Margarine

Unsweetened Chocolate

All-Purpose Flour

Salt

Vanilla

Peppermint Ice Cream

Chocolate Syrup

Maraschino Cherries

Miniature Marshmallows

Whipped Cream

Chopped Nuts

Candy Canes

For a large gathering, line Wilton's Treetliteful Pan with plastic wrap and pack firmly with a tangy cheese spread. Refrigerate. Unmold and trim with fresh rosemary sprigs and pimento stars. Merry munching!

Brownie À La Mode

4 Large Eggs

2 Cups Sugar

1 Cup Butter or Margarine

4 Ounces Unsweetened Chocolate

1½ Cup All-Purpose Flour

1 Teaspoon Salt

2 Teaspoons Vanilla

½ Gallon Peppermint Ice Cream

Chocolate Syrup

Maraschino Cherries

Miniature Marshmallows

Whipped Cream

Chopped Nuts

Candy Canes

Preheat oven to 325°F. Spray pan with non-stick vegetable spray. In a medium bowl, beat eggs; blend in sugar. Melt butter or margarine and chocolate in heavy saucepan over low heat or in microwave-safe container at medium (50%) power, stir. Blend chocolate mixture into sugar mixture. Add flour, vanilla and salt; stir (do not beat) until well mixed. Spread batter in prepared pan. Bake 25-35 minutes or until toothpick inserted in center comes out clean (do not overbake). Cool brownies in pan 10 minutes on a rack. Loosen at edge and turn out on rack to cool completely. Cover cake board with Fanci-Foil Wrap. Transfer brownie tree to prepared board. To serve, top with scoops of ice cream. Decorate your brownie tree sundae as desired. Suggested toppings: whipped cream, maraschino cherries, miniature marshmallows, chopped nuts, chocolate syrup, candy canes, Wilton nonpareils.

Makes 12 servings.

Substitute your favorite large batch brownie mix for a quick baking alternative. Ice cream scoops can be placed on a cookie sheet and frozen 1-2 days ahead of serving.

TIME SAVER • TIP

DIVINE
DESSERTS

Simply stated, these heavenly sundaes will have you
in and out the kitchen in a twinkling!

CHECKLIST

DESSERT SHELLS
Wilton Products
Mini Star Pan

Ingredients
Flour Tortillas or Round
Frozen Waffles
Butter
Sugar
Cinnamon

CARAMEL SAUCE
Ingredients
Caramels
Whipping Cream
Optional, Instant Coffee Powder
OR Coffee Liqueur

Make your kids see "stars"! Use
Wilton's Mini Star Pans to create
Fanciful Popcorn Stars. Add mini
chocolate chips, gum drops or
nuts to your favorite popcorn
ball recipe. Line mold with
plastic wrap. Firmly
press in mixture.
Unmold.

Ice Cream Shells

6 Small (6 in.) Flour Tortillas or
6 Round Frozen Waffles
2 Tablespoons Butter, Melted
2 Tablespoons Sugar
$1^{1}/_{4}$ Teaspoon Cinnamon

Preheat oven to 400°F. For Tortillas: Warm slightly
in microwave to soften. For Waffles: Defrost and flatten by
rolling with a rolling pin.

Brush tops with melted butter. Sprinkle with cinnamon and
sugar. Spray Mini Star Pan with vegetable pan spray. Press
waffle or tortilla into pan. Push into points of star. Bake for
10-15 minutes or until crisp and lightly browned. Cool and fill
with ice cream or pie fillings. Garnish with whipped cream.

Makes 6 shells.

Caramel Sauce

7 Oz. Caramels
$1/_2$ Cup Whipping Cream

$1/_2$ Teaspoon Instant Coffee
Powder OR 1 Tablespoon
Coffee Liqueur, Optional

Place all ingredients, except liqueur, in a microwave-safe
bowl or heavy saucepan. Microwave or cook on medium heat
for 7-8 minutes, stir frequently. Cook until smooth. Serve
warm or cool over ice cream.

Makes $1^{1}/_{4}$ cups sauce.

CHERRY
SANTA

This Santa will shine as the star of your holiday table!

Delectable Desserts

CHECKLIST

Wilton Products

Star Pan

Tip 21

Disposable Decorating Bags

Ingredients

Cherry Pie Filling

Whipped Cream or Non-Dairy Whipped Topping

Chocolate Chips

Cake

2 Cans (21 oz. each) Cherry Pie Filling, Drained

Chocolate Chips

Whipped Cream or Non-Dairy Whipped Topping

Bake and cool your favorite cake recipe or mix. Place on serving plate and cover with cherries. Using whipped topping in disposable bag and tip 21 pipe rosette eyes, nose, hat tassel and bottom star border. Add tip zigzag hat band. Pipe pull-out moustache. Position chocolate chip pupils.

Makes 12 servings.

Wilton's Star Pan can make your favorite quick-bread recipe special. Prepare two 9 x 5 loaf pan recipes of banana, cranberry or pumpkin bread. Pour into prepared Star Pan and bake. Festive!

THE LITTLE DRUMMER BOY

KATHER

LITTLE

DRUMMER
BEARS

Delightful
Decorating

Make your band of brownie lovers sing a merry tune!

Brownies freeze well. Bake these brownies up to one month ahead and freeze undecorated. They'll be ready to decorate when you need them! Be sure to wrap up airtight and thaw before decorating.

TIME SAVER · TIP

40

Bears

Favorite Brownie Recipe   **Buttercream Icing (pg. 54)**

Bake and cool brownies. Outline paws, face and ears with tip
4 strings. Add tip 4 dot paw pads, cheeks, inside ears.

Using icing, attach jawbreaker eyes and nose, licorice mouth,
large gumdrop hat. Attach licorice rims to marshmallow
drum. Pipe tip 18 string hat brim, tip 3 string criss-cross on
drum. Attach drum with icing.

For mallets, insert small gumdrop on the end of 2¹/₂ in.
pieces of spaghetti. Insert into bear.

Each serves 1.

41

Delightful Decorating

PARTY TRAIN!

All-on-board for Santa's North Pole Express—the sweetest holiday route.

CHECKLIST

Wilton Products

2-Pc. Choo-Choo Train Pan Set

Tips 4, 18, 21, 789

Standard Muffin Pan

Icing Colors: Lemon Yellow, Orange, Rose, Violet, Brown

Cake Board and Fanci-Foil Wrap

Santa Claus Icing Decorations

Rainbow Nonpareils Sprinkle Decorations

16 in. Featherweight Decorating Bag

Buttercream Icing (Recipe pg. 54)

Ingredients

Candy-Coated Chocolate Candies

Gum Drops, Spice Rings, Mini Round Hard Candies

Peppermint Discs, Mini Candy Canes, Large Gumball

Chocolate Stripe Cookies, Shredded Coconut

The Choo-Choo Train Pan bakes a 3-dimensional cake that will make your guests stop in their tracks. This 2-piece pan is right on time for dozens of occasions—birthdays, theme parties, school celebrations and more.

North Pole Express

6 Cups Firm-Textured Cake Batter

Bake train cake and one cupcake. Cool overnight for best results. Position on cake board. Using a 16 in. decorating bag and tip 789, pipe band of icing around bottom of cake. Ice top and window of cake smooth. Ice train "face" smooth and position candy for facial features then pipe tip 4 pull-out hair. Attach cupcake "smokestack" with icing and pipe tip 4 yellow zigzag on sides. Pipe tip 21 rosettes on top of cupcake; sprinkle with nonpareils and add large gumball. Pipe tip 18 purple* stripes on front side of train. Add tip 21 orange stars on engineer's cabin. Position Santa Icing Decoration in window. Pipe tip 21 zigzag for "cowcatcher" and position candy canes. Pipe tip 4 zigzag lines around edges of train and trim with candies. Pipe tip 4 mounds of icing on front of train, position peppermint candies. Pipe tip 4 dot on candies and add mini round candies. Pipe tip 21 orange rosette on cake top; pipe tip 21 white rosettes and add candy. Position cookie wheels. Flatten spice drops and position for back wheels. Pipe tip 21 rosettes on outside of wheels and add candies. Sprinkle coconut on base.

Makes 12 servings.

*Note: Mix violet and rose to make purple color.

42

TASTY TREE TWOSOME

Two festive firs you will have fun decorating and eating!

CHECKLIST

FOR FACE TREE
Wilton Products

Tips 2A, 9

2 Pc. Stand-Up Tree Pan Set

Cake Board, Fanci-Foil Wrap

Icing Colors: Black, Christmas Red, Leaf Green

6 Pc. Nesting Star Cookie Cutters

Ingredients

Buttercream Icing (p. 54)

Favorite Pound Cake Recipe

Pretzel Rods, Gum Drops

FOR BEAR TREE
Wilton Products

Tips 8, 32

Icing Color: Kelly Green

Teddy Bears Icing Decorations

Ingredients

Mini Candy-Coated Chocolates

Shredded Coconut

The Stand-Up Tree Pan Set bakes up fantastic trees in 3-D! Instructions for 6 great decorating ideas including fruit cake and cinnamon tree recipes are included with the pan.

Beary Tree:

Bake stand-up tree cake and cool overnight, for best results. Cover cake with tip 32 stars. Pipe tip 8 mounds for clouds. Attach bear icing decorations and candy-coated chocolates. Sprinkle coconut around base.

Each tree serves 12.

44

Firry Face Tree

Trace second smallest cookie cutter on cardboard, cut out and cover with Fanci-Foil Wrap. Cut pretzel rods in half and insert into cake for "arms".

Ice cake fluffy with spatula. Pipe tip 2A stripes on pretzel arms; pat and smooth with finger dipped in cornstarch. Add tip 2A dot fingers. Add tip 2A dot eyes, pupils and nose. Pipe tip 9 outline mouth and pipe-in black area with tip 9. Cut red gumdrop in half, press and shape into heart and position in mouth for tongue. Add gumdrops and position star.

45

Delightful Decorating

COMIC
CHRISTMAS
CHARACTERS!

Invite this trio to a kids' party and let the fun begin!

Cake

Prepare your favorite cake recipe or mix. Bake and cool mini ball cakes. Decorate faces as follows:

SNOWMAN
Ice fluffy. Position cut licorice pieces for mouth and eyes, candy corn for nose. Pipe tip 32 swirl hat, ending with a tip 21 star pom-pom.

SANTA
Add a small amount of red color to white icing to create pink face color. Ice smooth. Pipe tip 21 reverse shells for beard and hair on sides. Pipe tip 21 pull-out star moustache. Pipe tip 32 swirl hat, ending with a tip 21 star pom-pom.

ELF
Add a small amount of red color to white icing to create pink face color. Ice smooth. Pipe tip 12 pull-out ears and nose. Pipe a tip 3 line in green at base of cake; attach spearmint leaves to form collar. Position candy-coated chocolates for eyes; position wafers for cheeks. Pipe tip 32 swirl hat ending with tip 21 star pom-pom. Pipe tip 21 pull-out star brim. Pipe tip 3 string mouth.

CHECKLIST

Wilton Products

Mini Ball Pan

Tips 3, 12, 21, 32

Icing Colors: Kelly Green, Brown, Red-Red

Ingredients

Favorite Cake Recipe or Mix

Buttercream Icing (pg. 54)

Candy-Coated Chocolates

Spearmint Leaves

Licorice Bites

Candy Corn

Round Hard Wafer Candies

Throw a "snowball" at the kids this winter! Bake cakes in the Mini Ball Pan, ice pink or white and cover immediately with shredded coconut.

Follow these steps to help ensure your decorating stays perfect. Place cakes on cookie sheet, ice faces as stated above. Chill 30 minutes and transfer to Wilton doiles. Add remaining features.

TIME SAVER · TIP

COLORFUL
COZY
COTTAGE

Use this happy, holiday home as a charming centerpiece!

CHECKLIST

Wilton Products

Stand-Up Holiday House Pan
Tips 1M, 4
Cake Board
Fanci-Foil Wrap
Pink Cake Sparkles™

Ingredients

Buttercream Icing
Gingerbread Cake Mix
Mini Round Hard Candies
Large Spice Drops
Candy Cane Sticks
Round Hard Wafer Candy
Multi-Colored Rock Candy

Build your own dream house! The Holiday House Pan gives you so many decorating options—from a fresh bread bungalow to an elaborate gingerbread cottage. Easy instructions for 5 festive designs are included with pan.

Home Decoration!

2 Gingerbread Cake Mixes
Buttercream Icing (Recipe pg. 54)
Assorted Candies

Bake cake using 5 cups of batter and directions on Holiday House package. Cool. Trim bottom of cake, allowing it to stand level. Using tip 4, pipe door and window areas smooth with spatula. Add round wafers for windows and pipe tip 4 zigzag shutters and around door; add candies to door and windows. Pipe tip 4 zigzag at corners of house and attach candy canes. Pipe tip 1M on roof in a drop garland effect. Spatula-ice buttercream fluffy on board to resemble snow. Pipe tip 1M rosettes around base of board and add rock candy. Add spice drops and Cake Sparkles.

Makes 12 servings.

WONDERFUL
WINTER
WONDERLAND

Cozy cabins nestled in "snow" will have you
dreaming of a white Christmas!

CHECKLIST

Wilton Products

9 x 13 in. Sheet Pan

Pre-baked Gingerbread House
Ornament Kit

Tip 2

All Occasion Script Message
Press Set

Ready-To-Use Rolled Fondant
(2 pks. needed)

3 Pc. Spruce Tree Set
(2 pks. needed)

Cake Board

Fanci-Foil Wrap

Holly Icing Decorations

Ingredients

Favorite Cake Recipe or Mix

Buttercream Icing (pg. 54)

Peppermint Sticks

These houses look great hanging
from your tree, too! The Wilton
Pre-baked Gingerbread House
Ornament Kit has all you need
to make two decorated houses.

Snowy Scene

Make gingerbread house ornaments following kit directions, omitting the hanging ribbons. Let dry. Prepare and
cover 1-layer cake with rolled fondant following package
directions. With remaining fondant, build up area on cake
top where one house will be positioned. Cover cake top
with imprinted messages. Ice snow areas on cake top
fluffy using buttercream icing. Tint icing using icing color
included in ornament kit and outline message using tip 2.
Position houses and trees on cake top.

Cut peppermint sticks to fit bottom border and attach with
dots of icing. Attach holly icing decorations to corners and
centers with dots of icing.

Makes 14 servings.

Delightful Decorating

VERY MERRY
MINI
CAKES

To each his own—sweet, single-sized servings sure to satisfy!

Singles Cakes

Prepare favorite cake recipe or mix. Spray Singles!™ Molds with vegetable cooking spray. Pour mixture into molds and bake. One cake mix makes 12-14 cakes. Cool and decorate.

For Candy Canes: Ice cakes smooth. Position licorice string "stripes".

For Stockings: With spatula, ice stocking fluffy. Pipe tip 32 swirls to form cuff. Pipe tip 3 string stitching on toe and heel. Attach candy and pick to top.

Each mini cake serves 1.

CHECKLIST

Wilton Products
CANES
Singles!™ Candy Cane Mold

STOCKINGS
Singles!™ Stocking Mold
Tips 3, 32
Kelly Green Icing Color
Jolly Santa Fun Pix

Ingredients
CANES
Red Shoestring Licorice

STOCKINGS
Assorted Candies, Candy Canes, Candy Sticks

Fruit cakes baked in Singles!™ Candy Cane and Stocking Pans make ideal gifts for friends and neighbors. They can be made ahead and frozen. To give, wrap in colorful foil and tie with ribbon.

See pages 26 and 46 for hints on how to make icing small cakes easy.

TIME SAVER · TIP

Delightful Decorating

SEASON'S
BIRTHDAY
GREETINGS!

Have a "Very, Merry Birthday" with this colorful cake!

Cake

Bake and cool cake. Brush apricot glaze on cake and cover with rolled fondant tinted blue, following package directions. Pipe tip 12 zigzag snowbank border. Pipe tip 12 message. Add icing decorations at pan divisions and centered between divisions. Place jawbreakers on border and on letters. Pipe tip 13 star snowflakes on cake sides. Place candles around cake.

Buttercream Icing Recipe

½ Cup Solid Vegetable Shortening
½ Cup Butter or Margarine*
1 Teaspoon Clear Vanilla Extract

4 Cups Sifted Confectioners' Sugar (Approximately 1 lb.)
2 Tablespoons Milk**

Cream butter and shortening with electric mixer. Add vanilla. Gradually add sugar, one cup at a time, beating well on medium speed. Scrape sides and bottom of bowl often. When all sugar has been mixed in, icing will appear dry. Add milk and beat at medium speed until light and fluffy. Keep icing covered with a damp cloth until ready to use. For best results, keep icing bowl in refrigerator when not in use. Refrigerated in an airtight container, this icing can be stored 2 weeks.

Makes 3 cups.

*Substitute all-vegetable shortening and ½ teaspoon Wilton Butter Flavor for pure white icing and stiffer consistency.

**Add 3-4 tablespoons light corn syrup per recipe to thin for icing cake.

Apricot Glaze

Heat 1 cup of apricot preserves to boiling, strain, then brush on cake while still hot. It will dry to a hard finish in 15 minutes or less. Ideal for crumb-coating cakes before icing.

CHECKLIST

Wilton Products

Happy Birthday Pan

Tips 12, 13

Royal Blue Icing Color

Cake Board, Fanci-Foil Wrap

Ready-To-Use Rolled Fondant (1 pk. needed)

Icing Decorations: Petite Wreath, Snowman and Christmas Tree

Candystick Candles

Ingredients

Mini Jawbreakers

Apricot Glaze

Buttercream Icing

Make birthday breakfast memorable using Wilton's Happy Birthday Pan to create party pancakes. Follow recipe on page 10 and garnish letters with jelly or sprinkle pancake with powdered sugar.

54

K R I S
KRINGLE
CAKE

Make merry holiday memories with this jolly, easy cake!

CHECKLIST

Wilton Products

Smiling Santa Pan

Red-Red Icing Color

5-Pc. Confectionery Tool Set

Ready-To-Use Rolled Fondant
(1 pk. needed)

Cake Board

Fanci-Foil Wrap

Ingredients

Candy-Coated Chocolates

Favorite Cake Recipe or Mix

Our Ready-to-Use Rolled
Fondant is easy to shape
into any holiday form.
Make holly and
berries, ribbons and
pointsettias — just
tint fondant and
shape. An easy
way to make an
impressive cake!

Fondant Santa Cake

Candy-Coated Chocolates   Favorite Cake Recipe or Mix

Prepare favorite cake recipe or mix. Bake and cool completely.
Brush with apricot glaze (see page 54). Tint a 1^1/$_4$ in. ball of fondant
light pink for face (using just a little red-red color) and a 1 in. ball
for nose; tint a 2^1/$_2$ in. ball of fondant red-red for hat and mouth.
Be sure to keep each piece of fondant tightly wrapped in plastic
wrap or in a closed plastic bag. Fondant dries quickly when uncov-
ered. Leave remainder white. (Use the outside of pan as a guide to
shape fondant face, beard, mouth and hat. Position fondant pieces
on cake; smooth. Add nose. Roll a ^{1}/$_2$ in. x ^{1}/$_2$ in. piece of fondant
for eyebrows; use veining tool to make impression lines on eyebrows; position. Shape fondant on pan for mustache; place on cake
and use veining tool in confectionery set to add score lines. If
fondant pieces do not hold together, add a small drop of water
to attach brows, mustache and eyes.

Makes 12 servings.

Because fondant keeps cakes moist, it's
perfect for decorating cakes a few days
ahead of the party. Store
your cake at room
temperature for
2-3 days.

TIME SAVER · TIP ·

NICE 'N NUTTY TREATS

Colorful Candy & Cookies

Two merry munchers sure to please family & friends!

Candy Melts wafers melt quickly in your microwave or double-boiler — easy for molding holiday candies.

Rocky Road Treats

1 (14 oz.) Package Wilton Lt. Cocoa Candy Melts

1½ Cups Mini Marshmallows

¾ Cup Pecans or Walnuts

Follow melting instructions on Candy Melts package. Add remaining ingredients and mix. Spoon into clean, dry Singles! mold. Top with additional marshmallows and nuts if desired.

Makes 4 shapes.

Orange Pecans

1 Tablespoon Wilton Meringue Powder

3 Tablespoons Water

¾ Cup Sugar

¾ Teaspoon Cinnamon

¼ Teaspoon Cardamom

1 Tablespoon Grated Orange Peel (About 3 Oranges) or 1½ Teaspoons Dried Orange Peel

⅛ Teaspoon Salt

8 oz. Pecan Halves

Preheat oven to 275°. Line cookie sheet with aluminum foil, spray with vegetable cooking spray. Lightly beat meringue powder with water in large bowl. Add sugar, orange peel, cinnamon, cardamom and salt, stir well. Stir in nuts until evenly coated. Spread out on prepared pan. Bake 30-35 minutes or until crisp, stirring occasionally. Recipe may be doubled.

You may omit orange peel and cardamom and increase cinnamon to 1 teaspoon and add ⅛ teaspoon allspice.

Orange Pecans may be made two weeks in advance and stored at cool room temperature in an airtight container. Store Rocky Road Treats in a loosely covered container.

TIME SAVER · TIP

SANTA'S
CANDY
CARGO

Deliver the season's sweetest greetings with these candy-filled sleighs!

CHECKLIST

SLEIGHS

Wilton Products

Foil Petite Loaf Baking Cups

Candy Melts®*: Green, Red, White, Light Chocolate, Dark Chocolate (1 bag each needed)

Disposable Decorating Bags

Spatula

Ingredients

Candy Canes, Tape

CANDY CARGO

Wilton Products

Santa Face Candy Mold

Candy Melts®*: White, Light Cocoa

Candy Colors Set

Disposable Decorating Bags

Ingredients

Mini Pretzel Twists, Peanuts, Waxed Paper

Make it sweet and simple—candy, that is! Wilton's Candy Melts® make it deliciously easy and our Candy Molds create beautifully detailed shapes. You'll have a hard time choosing from the dozens of multi-shaped molds.

Sleighs

Place two foil liners together, tape outside corners of liners in place to prevent stretching. Melt candy according to package directions. Use spatula to "paint" inside of liner with melted candy. Place in freezer to set, about 10 minutes. Repaint and freeze again to set, about 15 minutes. Remove and carefully peel off foil liner.

Trim 1/2 in. off curved end of candy cane. Melt candy in disposable bag. Turn candy sleigh upside down and attach cane with melted candy. Let set. Fill sleigh with nut clusters, molded candy and candy-coated pretzels.

Candy Cargo

SANTA CANDIES

Make facial features and hat first with tinted white candy, melted and piped in mold with disposable bag with tip cut off. Refrigerate to set about 10 minutes. Fill in beard area and tassel with melted white candy. Refrigerate to set.

NUT CLUSTERS

Mix nuts in melted cocoa candy. Spoon onto waxed paper and refrigerate to set.

CANDY PRETZELS

Dip pretzels into melted white candy. Refrigerate to set. Pipe red and green lines with melted candy in disposable bag with tip cut off.

*brand confectionery coating

HOME
SWEET
HOME

Colorful Candy & Cookies

When you raise the roof on this house, you'll get a sweet surprise!

CHECKLIST

Wilton Products

Cozy Cottage Candy Making Kit

Christmas Lollipop Candy Mold

Candy Melts®: Lt. Cocoa, White, Red (1 bag each for molding candies to fill house)

Cake Board, Fanci-Foil Wrap

Disposable Decorating Bags

Rainbow Nonpareils Sprinkle Decorations

Ingredients

Mini Pretzel Twists, Ground Nuts, Candy-Coated Chocolates, Coconut, Crispy Rice Cereal, Jelly Trees

The Cozy Cottage Candy Making Kit has everything you need to mold a dazzling candy chalet—including molds, bags, Candy Melts, and meringue powder for making royal icing (just add confectioners' sugar).

Candy House

Mold house sections following kit directions. Refrigerate to set. Assemble house walls using melted Candy Melts. Let set. Assemble roof pieces together, then chimney pieces; let set. Set aside roof.

Mold candies for inside of house using various colors of Candy Melts and adding nuts, nonpareils, coconut or crispy rice after filling molds. Refrigerate to set.

Attach assembled walls to covered board with melted candy. Attach jelly trees to walls. Pipe Lt. Cocoa path and White snow around house, using cut disposable bag. Position pretzels, then candy-coated chocolates. Pipe snow on house, roof and pretzels. Let set.

Fill house with molded candies. Position roof.

Fill your candy house with purchased candies and truffles, instead of making candy.

TIME SAVER • TIP

for
Nick

LOLLIPOP
GUILD

Colorful Candy & Cookies

Stuff the kids' stockings with these
lickable, likeable chocolate charmers!

Candy

2 (14 oz.) Packages Light
Cocoa Candy Melts

1 (14 oz.) Package White
Candy Melts

Melt candy following package directions. Be sure
pan is completly dry, wipe cavities well with cloth.
Pour melted candy into center of pan cavities. Tap
pan gently on counter to break up bubbles and
spread candy evenly. Coating should be about $1/4$
inch thick. Place pan in refrigerator for approximately
10-15 minutes. Unmold onto hand or soft towel (tap
pan gently if necessary). Attach to sticks with melted
candy. Pipe in details in cut disposable bags — hair,
buttons, facial features, clothing outlines. Attach
candy trims with melted candy.

Makes 12.

CHECKLIST

Wilton Products

Mini Gingerbread Boy Pan

Candy Melts®— White, Lt. Cocoa

4 Pc. Candy Colors Set

$11^{3}/4$ in. Party Sticks

Disposable Decorating Bags

Ingredients

Candy-Coated Chocolates

Hard Candy Wafers

Candy Canes

Candy Packages

Starlight Mints

Gum Drops

Gift Box

Use the Gingerbread Boy Pan to
make cute mini cakes or brownies.
Ice and decorate
as desired. Why
not personalize
them for a
special party?

CHRISTMAS
CANDY
COLLAGE

Colorful Candy & Cookies

Celebrate the season with a creative combination of candies!

Our versatile, creamy candy melts are ideal for all your candy-making needs. Try dipping dried fruit pieces for an easy, sweet treat!

Colorful Candy

Mold candy shapes following directions on Candy Melts packages. Decorate as follows: See page 64 for molding tips and times.

LARGE TREES: Mold in Singles!™ Christmas Tree Mold, using Light Cocoa Candy Melts. Refrigerate to set and unmold. Spread melted White Candy Melts over top, then immediately decorate with Nonpareils, Mini Wreaths and pillow candy.

WREATHS: Mold in Singles!™ Fancy Ring Mold, using Green Candy Melts. Refrigerate to set and unmold. Drizzle with remainder of Green melts and immediately sprinkle with Holly Mix Sprinkle Decorations. Roll out spice drops for bows, using one drop for each side and one half drop for center.

CANDY CANES: Prepare Candy Cane recipe below and mold in Singles! Candy Cane Mold. After unmolding, drizzle with melted White and Red Candy Melts.

BITE-SIZE TREES: Fill Petite Tree Pan cavities halfway with melted White Candy Melts. Refrigerate to set. Fill to top of cavity with a layer of Red or Green Candy Melts. Refrigerate to set. Unmold and drizzle with melted candy.

Candy Cane Recipe

1 Pk. Each of White and Red Candy Melts

½ Teaspoon Peppermint Flavor (From Wilton Candy Flavor Set)

3 Candy Canes, Crushed

1 Cup Toasted Coconut

Add a small amount of melted Red to melted White Candy Melts. Add remaining ingredients and mold as directed.

SENSATIONAL
SHORTBREAD
SHAPES

CHECKLIST

Wilton Products

Cookie Molds:
Santa, Nutcracker, Stocking

Icing Colors:
Green, Orange, Red-Red

Candy Melting Plate

Decorator Brush Set

Cake Sparkles™

Clear Vanilla Extract

Ingredients

Butter

Confectioners' Sugar

Vanilla Extract

Flour

Salt

Cookie Molds aren't just for cookies! Create a wonderful clay gift plaque, using colorless art clay and instructions on the package. Paint in your favorite holiday colors.

Make our merry, molded cookies, then perk them up with an icing color "paint job"!

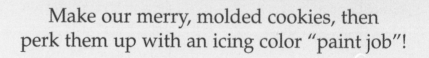

Shortbread

1 Cup Butter	2-2¼ Cups Flour
⅔ Cup Confectioners' Sugar	⅛ Teaspoon Salt
2 Teaspoons Vanilla Extract	

Preheat oven to 325°. In a medium mixing bowl cream butter, sugar and vanilla. Add flour and mix until dough is smooth. If dough feels sticky add additional ¼ cup flour as needed. Dough should be soft but not sticky. Spray cookie mold lightly with vegetable pan spray. Flour mold, shake out excess.

68

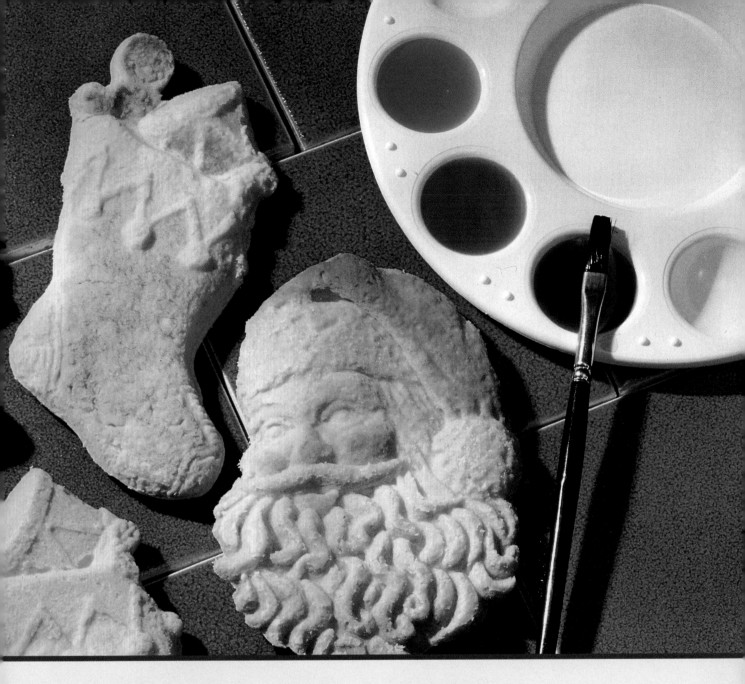

Firmly press dough into mold, making sure dough is even in mold. Prick surface with a fork. Bake in mold 30-35 minutes or until lightly browned. Cool in mold 10 minutes on rack. Loosen edges with tip of knife and flip mold over onto cutting board.

To paint cookies, dilute Wilton Icing Colors with a little clear vanilla extract. Place colors in Candy Melting Plate. Paint cookies when cooled. Sprinkle on Cake Sparkles for added holiday dazzle.

Makes 4-6 cookies.

Alternative Baking

Follow previous instructions, baking at 350°.

To make more than one cookie at a time; lightly oil mold and heavily flour. Press dough firmly and evenly into mold. Prick cookie. Strike edge of mold sharply on wooden cutting board 4-5 times. Rotate mold and strike again. Dough should come out. Place on cookie sheet. With thin pastry brush, brush off excess flour from cookie. Reflour mold before each cookie. Repeat with remaining dough. bake 15-20 minutes. Cool on rack. These cookies will not be as defined as cookies baked in the mold, as pictured.

CLEVERLY QUICK COOKIES

Who'd ever guess the secret of these cookies' success?

CHECKLIST

Wilton Products

Wilton Green Sugar

Wilton Red Sugar

Mini Gingerbread Boy Pan

Mini Tree Pan

Tip 3

White Tube Decorating Icing

Cinnamon Candies

Cookie Cutters

Ingredients

Refrigerated Sugar or Peanut Butter Cookie Dough

Confectioners' Sugar

Why have just plain cookies, cakes and candies, when you're just a sprinkle away from fancy? Choose from Wilton's wide variety of sprinkle decorations to perk up your treats!

Easy Holiday Cookies

TIME SAVER • RECIPE

Looking for a way to "jump-start" your holiday baking? Why not try the magic combination of refrigerated cookie dough and Wilton. Our cutters, holiday-shaped pans, sprinkles and baking sheets will have you baking like a pro in no time. Sprinkle sugars on cut-out cookies before baking, or, sprinkle and then roll out and cut. Follow baking directions on package.

TREES AND GINGERBREAD BOY

Spray Mini Tree or Gingerbread Boy pans with vegetable pan spray. Press about 2 teaspoons dough (peanut butter for gingerbread boy and sugar for trees.) in each cavity. Bake 10-15 minutes or until edges are light brown. Cool in pan for 5 minutes then remove, if necessary use a small spatula around edge. When cool, sprinkle trees with confectioners' sugar. Decorate gingerbread boys with white icing.

DROP COOKIES

Roll 2 teaspoons dough into ball, roll in red or green sugar. Place on ungreased cookie sheet and bake at 350°F for 10-12 minutes. Cool 5 minutes and remove from sheet.

COOKIE
COLORFEST

Colorful Candy & Cookies

Let the kids brush-up on their "cookie-coloring" skills with this project!

CHECKLIST

Wilton Products

Perimeter Cookie Cutters:
6-Point Star, Snowman, Stocking, Snowflake, Gingerbread Boy, Wreath

Paste Icing Colors

Cake Sparkles

Meringue Powder

Ingredients

Butter or Margarine

Sugar

Egg

Vanilla Extract

Baking Powder

Flour

Wilton offers a wide variety of cookie cutters for all occasions. They make your favorite cookie recipes look outstanding. Purchase extra cutters for the kids to use with clay or sand. Also, tie them on packages as gift trim.

Creative Cookies

1 Cup Butter or Margarine, Softened
1 Cup Sugar
1 Large Egg

1 Teaspoon Vanilla
2 Teaspoons Baking Powder
3 Cups Flour

Preheat oven to 375°F. In large bowl, cream butter and sugar with electric mixer. Beat in egg and vanilla. Add baking powder; add flour, one cup at a time, mixing after each addition. Dough will be very stiff; blend last flour in by hand. Do not chill. Divide into 2 balls. On floured surface, roll each ball in a circle approximately 12 in. diameter and 1/8 in. thick. Dip cutters in flour before each use. Bake cookies on ungreased cookie sheet on middle rack of oven for 8-12 minutes or until cookies are lightly browned. Cool and ice with royal icing "paint", Cake Sparkles and tube decorating icing.

Royal Icing

3 Level Tablespoons Meringue Powder

6 Tablespoons Water

4 Cups Sifted Confectioners' Sugar (approximately 1 lb.)

Beat all ingredients at low speed for 7–10 minutes (10–12 minutes at high speed for portable mixer) until icing forms peaks. For "painting", thin icing with water until the consistency of thick paint. Color as desired. Paint cookies with a pastry brush and icing. Let dry, 2–3 hours. To paint in details, thin paste icing color with clear vanilla and apply with brush. When sprinkling with sparkles or sugar, add before icing dries.

Makes 2–3 dozen cookies.

Use refrigerated cookie dough & canned icing to keep preparation time to a minimum.

TIME SAVER · TIP

MARSHMALLOW
MELT-A-WAYS

Create these creamy, dreamy cookie/candy combos!

Colorful Candy & Cookies

CHECKLIST

Wilton Products

Tree Perimeter Cookie Cutter

Candy Melts®—Lt. Cocoa, White
(1 pk. each)

Rainbow Nonpareils, Christmas
Tree Mix Sprinkle Decorations

Ingredients

Buttercream Icing (p.54)

Butter

Sugar

Egg

Baking Powder

Flour

Milk

Vanilla Extract

Salt

Mini Marshmallows, Halved

You're guaranteed baking success when using our Even-Bake® Cookie Sheets. This insulated bakeware browns without burning. After baking, cool off with our Non-Stick Steel Grids.

Chocolate Marshmallow Trees

Cut, bake and cool cookies. Ice with buttercream and position marshmallow halves. Place cookies on cooling rack and cover with melted candy. Immediately decorate with Tree and Nonpareil Sprinkles; let set.

Sugar Cookies

$1/2$ Cup Butter	$1^3/4$ Cups Flour
1 Cup Sugar	1 Tablespoon Milk
1 Egg	$1/2$ Teaspoon Vanilla
1 Teaspoon Baking Powder	$1/4$ Teaspoon Salt

Preheat oven to 375°F. Cream butter and sugar, add egg and mix. Add remaining ingredients and mix until smooth. Refrigerate dough 2 hours. Roll out dough $1/8$ in. thick on lightly floured surface, dip cutters into flour before each use. Place on ungreased cookie sheet. Bake 12-15 minutes or until lightly browned. Place on cooling rack for 5 minutes, remove from sheet and cool.

Makes 18-24 cookies.

HOLIDAY
CRISPY TREATS

This fool-proof family project creates darling decorations or stocking-stuffers!

CHECKLIST

Wilton Products

Mini Ball Pan

Tip 18

Icing Colors: Orange, Sky Blue, Christmas Red, Kelly Green, Lemon Yellow

Meringue Powder

Ingredients

Royal Icing (p. 72)

Margarine

Mini Marshmallows

Marshmallows

Crisped Rice Cereal

Black Shoestring Licorice

Mini Candy-Coated Chocolates

Stage a decorating contest for a kids' party. Bake kid-sized cakes in Mini Ball Pan. Provide Wilton Tube Decorating Icings and Sprinkles, licorice, pretzels and other candies. Let the fun begin!

Ornaments

¹/₂ **Cup Margarine**

8 Cups Mini Marshmallows

12 Cups Crisped Rice Cereal

Wilton Icing Colors

Royal Icing (recipe pg. 72)

Melt margarine, stir in mini marshmallows until melted. Stir in icing color*, cereal and mix well. Spray Mini Ball Pan with non-stick vegetable pan spray. Press cereal mixture into pan. Unmold. Ice top of bottom half smooth; attach top half of ornament. Pipe tip 18 zigzag rim. Immediately press candy-coated chocolates into rim.

Cut licorice into 3 ¹/₂ in. lengths and fold into a "U" shape. Insert both ends into larger marshmallow center and attach marshmallow to top of ornament with icing.

Makes 8 ornaments. Not suitable for hanging from tree.

*Make batches of various colors to create solid and two-toned ornaments.

Use tweezers to add tiny candies to ornaments with ease. You can position candies right where you want them, without harming your ornament.

D Y N A M I C

COOKIE
DUO

This tasty two-some is sure to be a hit with your "cookie crowd"!

CHECKLIST

POTATO CHIP COOKIES
Wilton Products
Petite Tree Pan

Rainbow Nonpareils

Ingredients
Butter

Sugar

Flour

Vanilla

Potato Chips

Buttercream Icing (p. 54)

PEANUT BUTTER SPRITZ
Wilton Products
13 Pc. Spritz Cookie Press Set

Tube Decorating Gels: Red, Green

Ingredients
Vegetable Shortening

Peanut Butter

Granulated Sugar, Brown Sugar

Egg

Vanilla Extract

Flour

The Spritz Cookie Press Set features 12 disks with holiday shapes. The easy-to-use Press is great for cookies and appetizers!

Potato Chip Cookies

1 Cup Butter, Softened	1 Teaspoon Vanilla
1/2 Cup Sugar	1 Cup Finely Crushed Potato Chips
1 3/4 Cups Flour	

Preheat oven to 350°F. Spray pan with vegetable pan spray. Cream butter and sugar until light and fluffy. Add flour and vanilla; mix well. Stir in potato chips. Press dough into cavities of pan, filling 1/4 in. from the top. Bake 12-15 minutes or until lightly browned. Cool 5 minutes in pan and remove to cooling rack. Decorate with Buttercream Icing and Rainbow Nonpareils.

Makes 3-4 dozen.

Peanut Butter Spritz

1/2 Cup Solid Vegetable Shortening	1 Egg
1/2 Cup Peanut Butter	1/2 Teaspoon Vanilla
1/2 Cup Granulated Sugar	1 1/2 Cups Flour
1/2 Cup Packed Brown Sugar	

Preheat oven to 375°F. In a large mixing bowl, cream together shortening and peanut butter. Gradually add sugars, blending well. Add egg, beating until smooth. Add vanilla. Set aside. Stir flour into peanut butter mixture. Place dough into cookie press and press cookies onto ungreased cookie sheet. Bake 6-8 minutes or until lightly browned around the edges. Remove cookies from sheet; cool on rack. Decorate with red and green Tube Decorating Gels.

Makes 3-4 dozen cookies.

CHRISTMAS

COOKIE
CHARACTERS

Fun-to-eat, cookie treats perfect
for petite party-goers!

Use refrigerated cookie dough in
place of recipe. Decorate
with Wilton Tube
Icing and assorted
candies.

Cookie Pops

Roll-out Cookie Dough Recipe p. 82   Buttercream Icing Recipe p. 54
(Makes 15-18 pops)

Prepare Dough. Bake and cool cookies on sticks, according to instructions on pan.

For Santa: Bake in tree pan. Add a small amount of red color to white icing for pink face color. Lightly ice face area and hat with spatula. Pipe tip 8 circular motion beard. Pipe tip 2 string eyes. Add tip 6 dot nose and mouth; add pull out moustache. Pipe in tip 8 zigzag on hat brim. Add tip 8 swirl on top of hat. Sprinkle Cake Sparkles on beard. For Snowman: Ice cookie with spatula. Pipe tip 7 zigzag hat and outline brim. Insert pretzel sticks for arms; position chocolate chip eyes, mouth and buttons; candy corn nose. Add licorice scarf.

Each makes 1 serving.

SANTA'S

COLOSSAL COOKIE

Share this super-sized Santa with the family
or take to a school party!

CHECKLIST

Wilton Products

Smiling Santa Pan

Tips 12, 32

Red, White Cake Sparkles
(1 pk. ea.)

Cake Board

Fanci-Foil Wrap

Ingredients

Cookie Dough:
Flour, Butter, Sugar, Egg,
Vanilla Extract, Baking Powder,

Buttercream Icing (Recipe p. 54)

Candy-Coated Chocolates

Fruit Rolls

Gumdrops

Hard Candy Wafers

Add pizazz to the
kids' party punch bowl.
Use Wilton's Smiling
Santa Pan to create
a cute ice mold.
Fill with punch
ingredients and
freeze. Cool idea!

Santa Cookie

1 Cup Butter	1 Teaspoon Vanilla Extract
1 Cup Sugar	2 Teaspoons Baking Powder
1 Large Egg	3 Cups Flour

In a large bowl, cream butter and sugar with an electric mixer. Beat in egg and vanilla. Mix baking powder and flour, adding one cup at a time and mixing after each addition. The dough will be very stiff; blend last flour in by hand (if dough becomes too stiff, add water, a teaspoon at a time). Do not chill dough.

Bake cookie in greased pan at 375°F for 15 to 17 minutes. Cool and unmold cookie onto rack, or to give as a gift place on foil-covered board. Sprinkle heavily with red Cake Sparkles. Pipe tip 32 reverse shell hat brim; add tip 32 swirl pom-pom. Cut mouth from fruit roll and position. Pipe tip 32 pull-out and swirl moustache and beard. Pipe tip 12 shell eyebrows. Position candy eyes, gumdrop nose and wafer cheeks. Sprinkle white Cake Sparkles on beard.

Makes 12 servings.

To Santa

HOLIDAY
SKIERS

Jolly Gingerbread

Glide through the holiday with these jolly gingerbread kids!

Skiers

Using Royal Icing from kit, pipe on pre-baked gingerbread boys, tip 14 zigzag hat, band, cuffs at arms and legs. Pipe tip 4 dot eyes, nose, buttons, cheeks; tip 4 string mouth. Pipe tip 12 pull-out hat; tip 47 scarf. Attach licorice poles to hands and candy to licorice with tip 4 dots of icing. Let dry. Attach candy cane skis to legs and board. Prop up on craft blocks until dry.

* Note: Mix Rose and Purple Icing Colors together for purple shade.

Use Wilton's Gingerbread Kids Ornament Kit to create Holiday place cards. Use icing to write names of guests & decorate as desired. Let children join in the fun!

O·H-H-H-H
CHRISTMAS
TREE!

Making this terrific gingerbread tree is fun for your entire family.

CHECKLIST

Wilton Products

Tips 1s, 2, 3, 16, 21

Icing Colors: Christmas Red, Black, Orange, Kelly Green

5-Pc. Bite Size Christmas Cookie Cutter Set

Cake Circles

Fanci-Foil Wrap

Meringue Powder

Ingredients

Tree Bough Pattern, p. 96

Royal Icing Recipe, p. 72

Grandma's Gingerbread Recipe, p. 95

Candy Dots

Spice Drops

Wilton Meringue Powder is a safe substitute for egg whites in all kinds of recipes— from Lemon Meringue Pie to the traditional holiday yule log with meringue mushrooms.

Trim That Tree

Prepare gingerbread recipe, but roll out 1/8 in. thick. Using pattern, cut 5 tree boughs from gingerbread dough. Using Bite Size Cutters, cut 12 snowmen and 1 star. Bake all and cool.

Assemble tree on foil-covered cake circle. Pipe tip 16 line of icing along bottom and straight edge of tree bough sections. Position two sections by joining straight seams, hold in position a few minutes until icing begins to set. Repeat for remaining sections. Let set completely before further decorating.

Decorate snowmen: Using tip 3, outline and pipe in snowmen; smooth with finger dipped in cornstarch. Add tip 3 hat and scarf; tip 1s dot buttons, eyes and mouth; tip 2 pull-out dot nose.

Decorate tree: Cover center seams with tip 16 strings. Edge boughs with tip 16 "c" motion shells and position candy dots. Pipe tip 21 stars and position candy dots. Add tip 3 random dots. Outline gingerbread star with tip 16 and position dot candy; add tip 16 star center. Pipe tip 16 rosette on tree top and position star.

Spatula ice board around tree fluffy. Attach gingerbread snowmen and spice drops to board with additional dots of icing.

WINTER CHATEAU!

Turn your table into a "Winter Wonderland" with this snowy scene!

CHECKLIST

Wilton Products

Pre-Baked Gingerbread House Kit

Tip 16 (included in kit)

Rainbow Edible Glitter

Two 13 x 19 in. Cake Boards

Fanci-Foil Wrap

Santa Claus Icing Decorations

Royal Icing (Meringue Powder for one recipe included in kit)

Meringue Powder (one additional Royal recipe needed for decorating house)

Candy (all candy included in kit except candy canes)

Ingredients

Patterns (pg. 96)

Small Candy Canes

Colored Ice Cream Cake Cones

Sugar Cones

6 in. Ruler

Coconut

No matter what your level of decorating expertise, the Pre-Baked Gingerbread House Kit is a great starting point, with easy-to-follow directions. Why not build a "Log Cabin", birdhouse or Santa's Workshop? Let the whole family join in!

Chateau

At least two hours before decorating, assemble house following instruction sheet directions.

Once house is assembled and icing has set, remainder of exterior can be constructed. **To build turrets at corners of house,** use full-sized cake cones; trim approximately 1½ in. from bottom of sugar cone, also trim top point of cone to allow gumball to rest securely. Assemble with tip 16: pipe icing into upright cake cone and on edge of sugar cone. Place sugar cone on cake cone. **To build side steeples** on roof, trim top portion from cake cone and cut bottom on angle to fit flush against roof. Trim sugar cone to 1¼ in. and trim top point of cone. Attach to base and let dry. **For center steeple,** trim approximately 1 in. from bottom of cake cone, trim sugar cone to measure 3½ in. and trim top point from cone. Assemble with tip 16.

Trace window and door patterns with toothpick. Ice smooth. Outline with tip 16 zigzag and position cinnamon dots.

Pipe tip 16 zigzag around base of house front walk and around turrets. Add spice drops and cinnamon dots. Attach candy canes and gumballs with tip 16. Soften remaining icing with corn syrup as directed on package instructions to achieve a snow-like effect. Spatula ice roof, steeples and turrets. Trim roof line with gumballs. Sprinkle with glitter. Add coconut around base.

GINGERBREAD
FAMILY!

Gather your family and friends around this charming centerpiece!

CHECKLIST

Wilton Products

Giant Tree Cutter

4 Pc. Gingerbread Family
Cookie Cutter Set

Bite-Size Star Cookie Cutter

Tips 1, 2, 4, 32

Icing Colors: Kelly Green, Royal
Blue, Rose, Violet, Christmas Red,
Lemon Yellow, Black

Cake Board, Fanci-Foil Wrap

Meringue Powder

Ingredients

Gingerbread Mix

Royal Icing (pg. 72)

Mini Round Candies

Assorted Christmas Hard Candies

Black Shoestring Licorice

Candy-Coated Round
Chocolate Candies

Spice Drops

Confectioners' Sugar

Christmastime is family time—that's
why our Gingerbread Family Cutter
Set is a holiday tradition.
Decorate cookies to match
your own family mem-
bers. Be sure to make
extra—no one can resist
gingerbread (our favorite
recipe is included
with set)!

Gingerbread

1 (15$^{1}/_{2}$ oz.) Gingerbread Mix   Assorted Candies

Royal Icing (pg. 72)   Confectioners' Sugar

Prepare gingerbread cookie dough according to package
directions. Cut out cookies. Make cookie stands for each cookie
by cutting a square of dough (Tree, 3 in.; Adults, 2$^{3}/_{4}$ in.,
Children 1$^{1}/_{2}$ in.), then cutting dough on a diagonal to form two
triangles. Bake and cool cookies and stands. Ice tree fluffy with
spatula. Roll jelly candy flat and cut into star with cookie cutter;
position on tree top. Add candies. Write tip 2 message. For
adults: Pipe tip 2 string mouths, tip 4 swirl hair, zigzag trim,
dots and pipe-in bow tie. For kids: Pipe tip 1 string mouths, tip
2 swirl hair, zigzag trim, dots and pipe-in bow tie. Attach cookie
stands to backs of cookies with icing. Let dry.

Cut two 13 x 9 in. oval boards and cover with foil. Place tree
and people on board. Pipe tip 32 swirl mounds around edge of
board. Position licorice and attach candies with black icing
for lights.

CHARMING
CHRISTMAS
CHAPEL

Create a serene Christmas scene with this charming church!

CHECKLIST

Wilton Products

Gingerbread House Kit

Tips 2, 2B, 3, 4, 17, 47, 349

Icing Colors: Christmas Red, Kelly Green, Brown, Black, Royal Blue

2 Small Doves

Tube Decorating Gels—Blue, Yellow, Red, Orange

Wooden Dowel Rods

2–5 in. Grecian Pillars

Silver Fanci-Foil Wrap

Meringue Powder

Grandma's Gingerbread Recipe (pg. 95)

Ingredients

Royal Icing (pg. 72; set aside small amount to be thinned for painting)

Sugar Cones

Styrofoam Block (1 in. x 16 in. x 18 in.)

Confectioners' Sugar

Flour

Baking Soda

Salt

Ginger, Cinnamon, Nutmeg, Cloves

Shortening

Sugar

Unsulphured Molasses

Eggs

Gingerbread Church

Make gingerbread according to recipe.

Use patterns in kit to cut the following pieces: A (cut 2), B (cut 2), D (cut 2), P (cut 5*). *On 2 of the P pieces already cut, center pattern piece F at bottom and cut a triangle opening that will allow chimney to fit flush against peaked roof. For front dormer, cut another piece A from center peak down to middle, measuring $3^3/8$ in. from top. Cut 2 pieces $1^5/8$ in. x $5^1/4$ in. and 1 piece 1 x $5^5/8$ in. to support dormer. Bake, cool and allow to air dry at room temperature for 48 hours according to package directions.

CHRISTMAS
CHAPEL

TO MAKE TREES

Leave 2 sugar cones full size, cut 1 inch off
bottom of 2 cones, cut 2 inches off bottom of
4 cones. Cover all trees with tip 17 pull-out
stars. Let dry. For tree bases, cut 2 dowel rods
at 8 inches, 2 at 6 1/2 inches. Insert rods into
styrofoam covered with waxed paper. Cover
dowel rods with vertical rows of tip 17 lines.
Overpipe with tip 17 to achieve thickness of
trunk. Let dry.

Pipe tip 3 snow on trees. When dry, attach
with icing full-size trees to 8 in. trunks,
medium size trees to 6 1/2 in. trunks. Let set.

Using tip 349, pipe an overlapping leaf
garland around pillars. Let dry and add tip
2 dot berries. To make wreath, on waxed
paper pipe tip 349 overlapping leaves in a
1 1/2 in. diameter circle. Overpipe rows to give
dimension. Add tip 2 dot berries. Pipe in tip
2 bow. Let dry.

Ice sugar cone smooth with spatula for church
steeple. Let dry. Thin down royal blue icing
with water and paint doves. Let dry.

FOR STAINED GLASS WINDOWS

On sides and back pieces, trace pattern M for windows. Ice in royal icing, background area of windows smooth in white; let dry. Outline window
area and divide each into eighths with tip 3
strings. Fill in each area with decorating gel; dry
flat. On front piece, use pattern N to trace doors.
Ice smooth; outline with tip 4 strings. Cover sides,
front and back of chapel with tip 47 smooth side
up bands. Begin at bottom of each piece and
slightly overlap as you proceed to top. Let dry.
Add tip 349 leaf garland around windows, add tip
2 dot berries. Let dry.

FOR ROOF AND DORMER ROOF

Pipe tip 2B smooth side up horizontal bands.

Cover styrofoam for base with foil. Assemble chapel and steeple according to kit directions. Insert dowel rods inside of pillars and position in icing at front of chapel. Attach dormer pieces together, when dry attach bottom pieces to pillars. Add roof over dormer. Fill in seams with tip 17 triple lines. Attach steeple to roof. Fill in any gaps with icing. Position doves and wreath for front dormer with icing.

Ice board fluffy with spatula. Use spatula and icing to add snow effect to roof, eaves and steeple. Position trees. Dust with confectioners' sugar.

Grandma's Gingerbread Recipe

5 to 5¹/₂ Cups All-Purpose Flour	1 Tsp. Cloves
1 Tsp. Baking Soda	1 Cup Shortening
1 Tsp. Salt	1 Cup Sugar
2 Tsps. Ginger	1¹/₄ Cups Unsulphured Molasses
2 Tsps. Cinnamon	
1 Tsp. Nutmeg	2 Eggs, Beaten

Preheat oven to 375°F. Thoroughly mix flour, soda, salt and spices. Melt shortening in large saucepan. Cool slightly. Add sugar, molasses and eggs; mix well. Add four cups dry ingredients and mix well.

Turn mixture onto lightly floured surface. Knead in remaining dry ingredients by hand. Add a little more flour, if necessary, to make a firm dough. Roll out on a lightly floured surface to ¹/₄ in. thickness for gingerbread house pieces. Bake on cookie sheet for 10-15 minutes.

One recipe of this gingerbread dough will yield the gingerbread house shown here.

Note: If you're not going to use your gingerbread dough right away, wrap it in plastic and refrigerate. Refrigerated dough will keep for a week, but be sure to remove it 3 hours prior to rolling so it softens and is workable.

Make the Wilton Gingerbread House Kit a new holiday tradition for your family. The kit includes house patterns, 3 plastic people gingerbread cutters, disposable bags, decorating tips and a step-by-step instruction book.

95

CREDITS

Creative Director.............Richard Tracy

Food Editor....................Zella Junkin

Cake Designer.................Steve Rocco

Senior Cake Decorator....Susan Matusiak

Cake Decorators.............Mary Gavenda
Diane Knowlton
Nancy Suffolk Guerine
Judy Wysocki

Recipe Development........Lois Levine

Food Stylist.....................Lois Hlavac

Photography....................Kathy Sanders Studio
Peter Dean Ross Photographs

Photo Assistants..............Cristin Nestor
Carey Thornton

Copy Editor.....................Jeff Shankman

Associate Editor..............Frani Marek Janci

Writers............................Mary Ann Cuomo
Mary Enochs
Marita Seiler

Design Production...........Marek/Janci Design

Production Manager.........Laura Fortin

Production Coordinator....Mary Stahulak

Wilton products used in this book are available from your local Wilton dealer. You can also write or call Wilton, see information below.

USA
Wilton Industries, Inc.
Caller Service # 1604
2204 West 75th St.
Woodridge, IL 60517
Phone: 1-630-963-7100
Fax: 1-630-963-7299
Worldwide Web: www.Wilton.com

Canada
Wilton Industries, Canada, Inc.
98 Carrier Drive
Etobicoke, Ontario M9W 5R1
Canada L4V1R9
Phone: 416-679-0790
Fax: 416-679-0798
E-mail: WILTNCAN @ Interlog.com

England
Wilton Industries/Europe, Inc.
Unit 8, Axis/Hawkfield Business Park
Whitchurch,
Bristol BS14 OBY
England
Phone: 011-44-1179-465777
Fax: 011-44-1179-465888

Patterns for Enchanted Winter Chateau, pg. 88-89

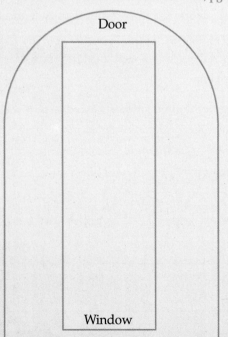

Door

Window

Pattern for Oh-h-h-h Christmas Tree!, pg. 86-87

Wilton CELEBRATE!

This Christmas collection of fabulous foods and sensational sweets is designed to put the "Happy" back in Holidays! You will have as much fun creating our taste-tempters, as you will have serving them. Look for the "Time-Saver Tip" or "Time-Saver Project" symbols throughout the book. These projects will have you out of the kitchen and into the party in a flash—another reason to CELEBRATE!

Festive Foods

Delectable Desserts

Delightful Decorating

Colorful Candy & Cookies

Jolly Gingerbread

Stock No. 2104-1227
ISBN No. 0-912696-51-6
Printed in Italy

Wilton Enterprises
2240 W. 75th Street
Woodridge, IL 60517
A Wilton Industries Company

0 70896 12271 1